MAGNiFiED!

MW01169762

KIDS ACTIVITY BOOK
FUN ACTIVITIES
FOR GRADES 1-4

MAGNIFY THIS!

Write your name on the handle of this magnifying glass.

Use your birthday month to decide what to draw inside the lens:

JANUARY, FEBRUARY, & MARCH
Draw something tiny that crawls.

APRIL, MAY, & JUNE
Draw something tiny that flies.

JULY, AUGUST, & SEPTEMBER
Draw something that would make you say, "Ouch!" if you stepped on it.

OCTOBER, NOVEMBER, & DECEMBER
Draw something you can find in your own backyard.

© 2024 Lifeway Press

ANT-TASTIC!

You were made for a f-ant-astic reason! To find it, work your way through the maze to the top of the anthill. Copy the letters you find along the path in the blanks below. Avoid letters on side paths trying to distract you!

Answer made to magnify God

THE BIG TRUTH: God created everything there is, and yet He still wants to spend time with me.

ZOOM IN: I am important to God.

BONUS VERSE: John 1:12

TODAY'S POINT: God sees me.

JESUS AND THE CHILDREN
John 1:1-3,12; Mark 10:13-16

Jesus was with God in the beginning when everything was created. Nothing was created without Jesus. God sent Jesus to earth to fix the relationship between God and people. One day, people brought their children to Jesus to ask Him to bless them. But Jesus' helpers tried to stop the parents. Jesus got very angry with His disciples and told them to let the children come. Then Jesus took the children in His arms and blessed them. Every person is important to Jesus. The Bible says that every person who receives the gift of salvation Jesus came to bring and believes in His name will be called God's child.

NOW YOU SEE IT!

This wrinkly round thing grows on a tree and has several names. Don't eat the fruit. The tree it grows on is sometimes used to make bows for arrows. Which name is not used for this fruit?

a. monkey brains   c. elephant skin
b. horse apple   d. hedge apple

Answer: c. elephant skin

Need to know the meaning of the words or ____? Just match each type of tree with the seed from which it grows.

PROCLAIM

to honor someone very highly

to tell about something important

MAGNIFY

to treat someone or something as very important

EXALT

Count the number of apple seeds. For each seed, think of a way you can magnify and exalt God.

BRANCH OUT!

3

DAY 2
MAGNIFY GOD'S CARE

THE BIG TRUTH: God keeps the whole universe going, and yet He still cares about what's happening to me.

ZOOM IN: I can trust God to take care of me.

BONUS VERSE: Deuteronomy 31:8b

TODAY'S POINT: God cares about me.

JESUS CALMED THE STORM
Mark 4:1,35-41

After teaching one day, Jesus used a boat to cross a lake with His disciples. A huge windstorm started. The boat started to fill up with water. Jesus was in the back of the boat asleep. The disciples woke Him up and said, "Teacher! Don't you care that we're going to die?" Jesus got up and commanded, "Silence! Be still!" The wind stopped blowing, and the water became calm! Then Jesus said to His disciples, "Why are you afraid? Do you still not have faith?" The disciples were terrified and asked each other, "Who then is this? Even the wind and the sea obey Him!"

NOW YOU SEE IT!

No hurry, but what's in the close-up photo above?

a. a fly's eye
b. a turtle's shell
c. a pineapple's skin
d. a beech tree's bark

Answer: b. a turtle's shell

WHAT'S HOP-PENING?

No matter what's hop-pening, God cares about you! Hop with your finger to the matching leaves, three of each, to find a Bible book, chapter, and verse. Then hop to it—find the verse in your Bible! How do these verses help you know that God cares about you?

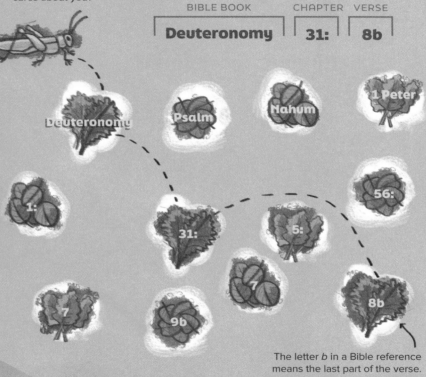

BIBLE BOOK	CHAPTER	VERSE
Deuteronomy	**31:**	**8b**

The letter *b* in a Bible reference means the last part of the verse.

BRANCH OUT!

Choose one of the verses. Think of three times you might need to remember the verse.

MAGNIFY GOD'S LOVE

THE BIG TRUTH: God is not OK with sin, and yet He still loves sinners like me.

ZOOM IN: I can be confident God loves me.

BONUS VERSE: Romans 5:8

TODAY'S POINT: God loves me.

THE WOMAN AT THE WELL

John 4:1-42

A Samaritan woman came to get water from a well where Jesus was resting. Jesus asked the woman to give Him a drink of water. Jesus talked to the woman. Then Jesus told the woman about ways she had disobeyed God. These were things that a stranger would not know about her. She recognized that Jesus was different. Jesus told her that He is God's promised Savior. The woman left her water jar at the well and went to tell other people in the town about Jesus, the Savior. Many Samaritans from that town at first believed in Jesus because of what the woman said. Later they believed because they heard Jesus for themselves.

NOW YOU SEE IT!

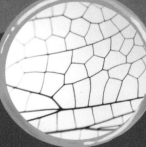

These can fly sideways and backwards! Have you seen one in your backyard!? It's a ...

a. spider web
b. flycatcher's wing
c. garter snake's scales
d. dragonfly's wing

Answer: d. dragonfly's wing

HOW MUCH IS THAT MUCH?

How much love and mercy does God have for people?
Find these Bible verses and write down your thoughts.

PSALM 103:11
How high? _____

_____

The word fear *means "awe or respect" here.*

PSALM 103:12
How far? _____

_____

_____

PSALM 107:1
How long? _____

_____

MICAH 7:19
How deep? _____

_____

_____

Iniquity is another word for "sin."

Finish this sentence five different ways:

God's love for me is as _____

as a _____.

BRANCH OUT!

7

PUDDLE PUZZLE

Drop in the correct letters to discover a marvelous thing Jesus did for you! Each pair of puddles will point you to the row and column where you can find the letter you need.

Answer: Jesus died on the cross as a substitute for anyone who believes.

J[ ]sus [ ] [ ] [ ] [ ]

on th[ ] cross [ ]s

[ ] subst[ ]tut[ ]

[ ]or

[ ] [ ] y o[ ] [ ] who

b[ ]l[ ][ ]v[ ]s.

Do you want to know more about why Jesus died and came back to life? Check out the last page in this booklet to learn more!

9

MAGNIFY GOD'S FORGIVENESS

THE BIG TRUTH: Jesus came to save the world, and that includes me.

ZOOM IN: I can trust Jesus as my Savior.

BONUS VERSE: John 3:16

TODAY'S POINT: God forgives me.

JESUS AND NICODEMUS

John 3:1-21; 18—20; 1 Corinthians 15:6

Nicodemus came to visit Jesus at night. Jesus taught Nicodemus that God loved the world by sending His only Son (Jesus). Jesus came to die to take the punishment for our sins so that we could have eternal life. Some time later, Jesus was arrested. Jesus never did anything wrong. And yet He was arrested unfairly. Jesus was crucified and died on a cross. Nicodemus helped prepare Jesus' body to be buried. After three days, some women went back to the tomb where Jesus had been buried. It was empty! Jesus had risen from the dead. Jesus rose from the dead so that those who receive His gift of forgiveness can be part of God's family forever.

NOW YOU SEE IT!

This fun fungus may boost people's immune systems. It's called:

a. turkey tail

b. pine petal

c. bloom's mushroom

d. dog's bark

Answer: a. turkey tail

PETAL POWER

What does it mean to repent? Find the answer in this field of flowers. The words you need are on the flowers with five petals. Rearrange those words and write them in the blanks below.

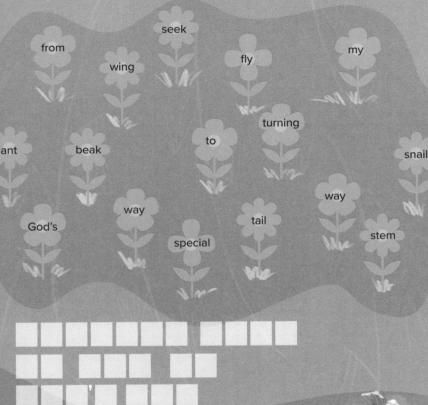

from
seek
wing
fly
my
turning
to
ant
beak
snail
way
God's
tail
special
way
stem

Give an example of following your way instead of God's way. Then flip-flop it! Give an example of following God's way instead of your way.

BRANCH OUT!

MAGNIFY GOD'S FAITHFULNESS

THE BIG TRUTH: God is faithful with the big things in my life, and He will be faithful with the small things too.

ZOOM IN: I don't have to worry because God keeps His promises.

BONUS VERSE: Psalm 100:5

TODAY'S POINT: God keeps His promises.

JESUS TAUGHT ABOUT WORRY

Matthew 6:25-34

One day, Jesus sat down on the side of a mountain and taught about what people should do when they worry. Jesus knew that people worry about many things, like having the clothes and food they need. He encouraged them to trust that God would provide for their needs. Jesus talked about everyday things like birds and flowers to help the people understand what He meant. He said, "If God cares about things as small as flowers and birds, you can trust that He cares about you, too. You are worth more than birds and flowers." The Bible is full of God's promises to provide what we need. God always has and always will keep His promises.

NOW YOU SEE IT!

You won't believe its eyes! This critter's eyes are so big, in some species you can see the eyes by looking in the ears! It's an ...

a. eagle
b. possum
c. owl
d. hawk

12

Answer: c. owl

REARRANGED RAINDROPS

When light hits tiny raindrops, it can make a giant rainbow with these colors: **red**, orange, yellow, **green,** blue, dark blue, and **purple**. Read the words next to each raindrop in this color order, then find the same promise in your Bible.

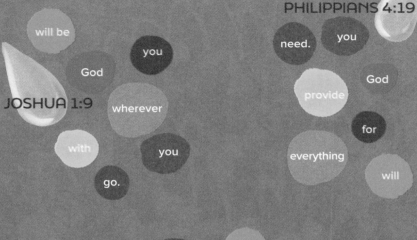

PHILIPPIANS 4:19

JOSHUA 1:9

will be
you
God
wherever
with
you
go.

need.
you
God
provide
for
everything
will

1 JOHN 1:9

will
forgive
God
to
be
faithful
sin.

What words would you add to the rainbow to explain this verse about God's faithfulness?
1 Corinthians 10:13

BRANCH OUT!

13

PLAN BEE

You've learned some amazing things about God at VBS. What do you plan to do now that you know them?

Use colored candies for playing pieces. Take turns placing a playing piece on the honeycomb. Bee-fore you can place a piece of candy, use the words on the honeycomb to fill in the first blank of this sentence:
If _____, then _____. Fill the second blank with how that truth will change how you think or act. (For example: "If God sees me, then I can have a relationship with Him.")

To bee-t your opponent, place three of your pieces in a straight row.

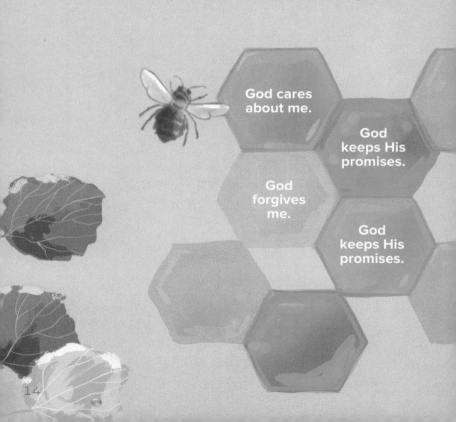

God cares about me.

God keeps His promises.

God forgives me.

God keeps His promises.

God sees me.

God cares about me.

God loves me.

God loves me.

God forgives me.

God forgives me.

God keeps His promises.

God cares about me.

God keeps His promises.

God sees me.

God sees me.

God loves me.

God sees me.

God forgives me.

God cares about me.

God loves me.

STARE...THEY'RE THERE!

Your eyes might go googly the longer you stare, but there are four important words on this page. Can you read them all? (Need a hint? Close your eyes and think about Psalm 34:3.)

Answer: magnify, proclaim, together, exalt